11.95

EVANSTON PUBLIC LIBRARY

3 1192 00903 5369

xBiog Jacks.J Marti.P

Martin, Patricia Stone.

Jesse Jackson : a
  rainbow leader /

MAY 0 1 1996

Jesse Jackson
A Rainbow Leader

Patricia Stone Martin

illustrated by Bernard Doctor

Rourke Enterprises Vero Beach, Florida

©1987 by Rourke Enterprises, Inc.

All rights reserved. No part of this book may be reproduced or utilized in any form or by any means, electronic or mechanical including photocopying, recording, or by any information storage and retrieval system without permission in writing from the publisher except for the inclusion of brief quotations in an acknowledged review.

Manufactured in the United States of America

Library of Congress Cataloging-in-Publication Data

Martin, Patricia Stone.
  Jesse Jackson -- a rainbow leader.

  (Reaching your goal biographies)
  Summary: Examines the life of the black leader and civil rights worker from his childhood to the present, describing how he achieved his goal of obtaining more rights for blacks.
  1. Jackson, Jesse, 1941-   – Juvenile literature.
2. Afro-Americans – Biography – Juvenile literature.
3. Civil rights workers – United States – Biography – Juvenile literature. [1. Jackson, Jesse, 1941-
2. Civil rights workers. 3. Afro-Americans – Biography]
I. Title. II. Series: Martin, Patricia Stone.
Reaching your goal biographies.
E185.97.J25M37 1987   973.92′092′4 [B] [92]   87-12897
ISBN 0-86592-170-9

Jesse wanted a drink of water. He saw a water fountain. "You can't drink from there," a man said.

Jesse stopped. "Why can't I?" he asked.

"Because only white people can drink from there," said the man.

Jesse did not think that was fair. He saw other things that were not fair. Some restrooms were only for white people. Some places to eat were only for white people. "When I grow up I will help change these things," said Jesse.

Today things *are* different. Jesse Jackson helped change them.

Jesse Louis was born on October 8, 1941, in Greenville, South Carolina. His mother was Helen Burns, and his father was Noah Robinson. When Jesse was almost two years old, his mother married a man named Charles Jackson.

As a boy, Jesse wanted to get things done. He did not think black people were treated fairly. When he was in high school, he led a protest. Marches and sit-ins are two kinds of protests. People protest to call attention to something they feel is wrong. Jesse wanted everyone to know that black people were not treated in the same ways as white people.

Jesse was very popular in high school. He was the quarterback of the football team. Jesse held class offices. While he was in high school, he was adopted by Charles Jackson.

After high school, Jesse was offered a job with the New York Giants. They wanted him to play baseball on the team. A white player was offered more money to play with the same team. Jesse knew that this was not fair. He decided not to take the job.

Instead, he went to the University of Illinois. The school had offered him a scholarship to play on its football team. But the team would not let Jesse play quarterback. The reason, Jesse was told, was that he was black.

Jesse changed schools. He went to an all-black school in North Carolina. He was a leader in his new school. He was also a star on the football team. While he was in school, he worked for people's rights. He thought everyone should have the same rights, whether they were black or white.

Jesse met a girl named Jacqueline Davis. He thought she was pretty, and he knew right away he wanted to marry her. She laughed at that. But in 1962 they were married.

Jesse was still unhappy with the way black people were treated. One summer he led a protest march down the main street of Greensboro. He was put in jail.

In 1965, Martin Luther King, Jr., went to Selma, Alabama. He led a protest march there.

King was an important black leader. The police fought with the marchers. Dr. King asked for help from other black people. Jesse Jackson came to Alabama to help him. Jesse brought other people with him. While he was there, Jesse gave his first big speech. The people liked what he said.

Selma, Alabama, was not the only place where black people were unhappy. They were unhappy in many cities and towns. And they were protesting in some of these places. Sometimes buildings were set on fire. Many people were hurt. People were angry. When Jesse talked to them, they calmed down.

White leaders thought Jesse was a good leader. He could talk to black people, and they listened to him.

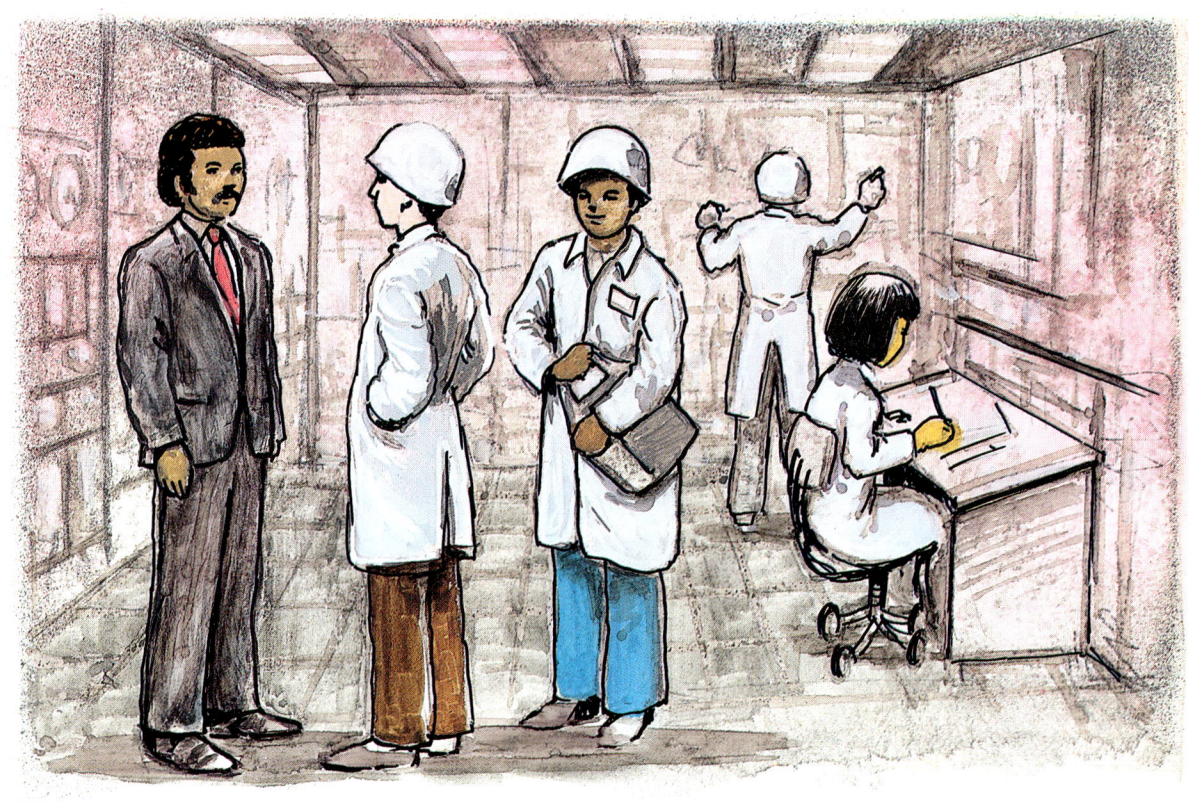

Jesse did not like the rules at some companies. They did not hire black people to work for them. Jesse told people not to buy anything from these companies. His idea worked. The companies lost money. Then they started to hire black people.

Dr. King decided to go to Chicago. He wanted to help black children get into all-white schools. He also wanted to get rid of the slums — the dirty, crowded places where many black people lived. Many black people in Chicago did not want Dr. King to come. They were afraid. Jesse talked to many preachers. Many of them met Dr. King at the airport when he arrived. They welcomed him to Chicago.

That summer, there were many fights in Chicago. It was hot, and people were upset. Dr. King talked to the white leaders in Chicago, but they did not change anything. So Jesse led marches through white neighborhoods. The white people did not like these marches. They became very angry. They threw stones at the marchers. Jesse was hit by a stone. Finally in August the mayor changed his mind. He said the city would clean up the slums.

In 1968, Dr. King went to Memphis. He led a protest march there. Again there was fighting. Jesse came to help. On April 4, Dr. King was killed. Jesse Jackson was with him.

Jesse returned to Chicago. He talked about Dr. King on the "Today Show." Some black people began to think of Jesse as their new leader.

Later that spring, the Poor People's March was held in Washington, D.C. People from all around the country came to march. Again fighting broke out, and Jesse helped to stop it.

On June 30, 1968, Jesse became a minister. He could now be called Reverend Jesse Jackson. He led many marches. One was a march against hunger. Jesse believed that all people should have food, including poor people.

In the 1970s, Jesse started a new program. He called it PUSH, short for People United to Save Humanity. The purpose of the program was to push for better educations for children. He wanted to push them to do their best. He wanted all children to say, "I am somebody."

Jesse saw many ways to help people. He wanted more blacks to vote. He wanted the government to spend more money on poor people. In November, 1983, Jesse said he would run for president.

The next month, an American pilot was shot down in Lebanon, a country almost halfway around the world. The leaders of Lebanon would not let the pilot come home. Jesse went there. He talked with the leaders. They let Jesse bring the pilot home with him.

Jesse became an American hero. President Reagan invited him to the White House. Everyone was proud of Jesse.

Jesse Jackson was not elected president. Some day he may run for president again. He has said, "I was born to lead." Jesse has reached many of his goals. He has helped change the lives of many people, black *and* white.

Reaching Your Goal

What are your goals? Here are some steps to help you reach them.

1. **Decide on your goal.**
   It may be a short-term goal like one of these:
   learning to ride a bike
   getting a good grade on a test
   keeping your room clean
   It may be a long-term goal like one of these:
   learning to read
   learning to play the piano
   becoming a lawyer

2. **Decide if your goal is something you really can do.**
   Do you have the talent you need?
   How can you find out? By trying!
   Will you need special equipment?
   Perhaps you need a piano or ice skates.
   How can you get what you need?
   Ask your teacher or your parents.

3. **Decide on the first thing you must do.**
   Perhaps this will be to take lessons.

4. **Decide on the second thing you must do.**
   Perhaps this will be to practice every day.

5. **Start right away.**
   Stick to your plan until you reach your goal.

6. **Keep telling yourself, "I can do it!"**

Good luck! Maybe some day you will become a leader like Jesse Jackson.

Reaching Your Goal Books

Beverly Cleary
She Makes Reading Fun

Bill Cosby Superstar

Jesse Jackson A Rainbow Leader

Ted Kennedy, Jr.
A Lifetime of Challenges

Christa McAuliffe
Reaching for the Stars

Dale Murphy
Baseball's Gentle Giant

Dr. Seuss We Love You

Samantha Smith Young Ambassador

Rourke Enterprises, Inc.
P.O. Box 3328
Vero Beach, FL 32964